# 1 2 3
## The counting book

illustrated by Peter Stevenson

CHANCELLOR
PRESS

This edition published 2003 by Chancellor Press,
an imprint of Bounty Books, a division of
Octopus Publishing Group Ltd,
2-4 Heron Quays, London E14 4JP

© Ward Lock Limited 1980

First published in Great Britain in 1980
by Ward Lock Limited, 47 Marylebone Lane,
London W1M 6AX, a Pentos Company.

House editor Lesley Young

Printed and bound in Great Britain by
Sackville Press Billericay Ltd

**British Library Cataloguing in Publication Data**

Stevenson, Peter
    Ward Lock's counting book.
    1. Numeration—Juvenile literature
    2. Numeration—Pictorial works
    I. Title
    513'.2    QA141.3

ISBN 0 7537 0745 4

One day a man went out to mow a meadow and on the way he saw...

**one rabbit
in its burrow**

# 2

two swans
in some reeds

# 3

three tractors at work

# 4

**four crows in a field**

# 5

**a boy with five fish**

# 6

six frogs in a pond

# 7

**seven moles
and seven molehills**

# 8

**eight trees
by the roadside**

# 9

**nine cows in a pasture**

# 10

and in the meadow
he found
ten sheaves of corn.

How many pigs do you see in the pen?
How many ears do they have?

**How many birds are sitting on the wire?**

# How many wasps are buzzing about?

How many ducks are flying past?

How many lambs has this sheep?
How many noses can you count?

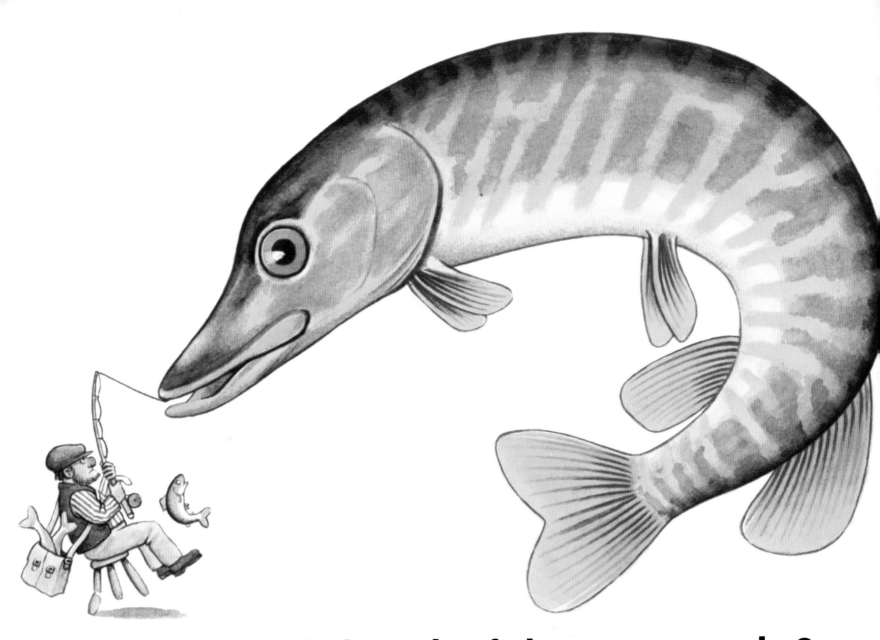

How many fish has the fisherman caught?

How many apples are on this tree?
How many green caterpillars can you find?

The end